SHARKS

What's inside?

TWO CAN

World of sharks

Many different kinds of sharks live in the ocean. Some sharks lurk on the ocean floor, others glide through the water looking for tasty animals to eat. All sharks swim by twisting their bodies from side to side.

whitetip reef shark

sand tiger shark

angel shark

grey reef shark

3

Great white shark

A great white shark looks so fierce that it has few enemies. Its huge jaws are packed with razor-sharp teeth that can snap up a dolphin or even another shark. Scientists think that great white sharks can live for more than 100 years.

How big?

A great white shark has bigger teeth than any other shark. Each tooth is about the same size as your hand.

ha ha

What do you get if you cross a snowball with a shark? Frostbite!

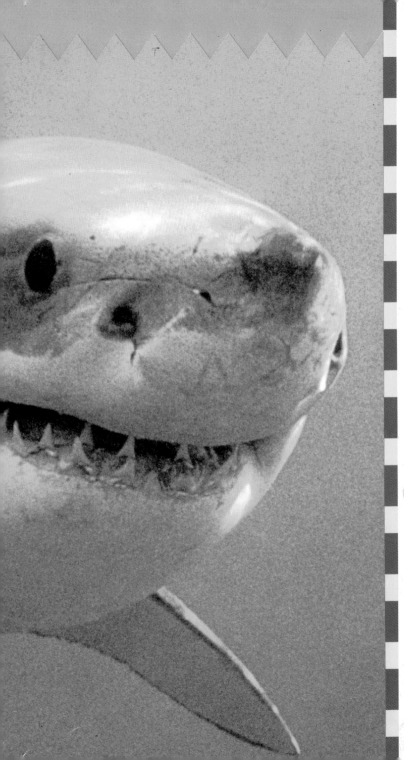

Great white sharks have been known to bite chunks out of boats. Perhaps boats look like food to a hungry shark!

A killer whale is the only animal in the sea that's brave enough to try to eat a great white shark.

A great white shark pokes its head above the water to see if there's anything to eat.

5

Terrifying teeth

Sharks' teeth come in all kinds of shapes and sizes. Some sharks have flat teeth to crush shells, others have spiky teeth to stab fish. The deadliest sharks have teeth shaped like knives to rip meat.

Dagger teeth

A speedy mako shark chases a shoal of fish. This scary beast can easily catch a fish between its dagger-like teeth and gulp it down whole.

Spit it out!

A shark bites things to find out if they are tasty. When a shark sinks its teeth into an old piece of junk by mistake, it spits out the junk and swims away.

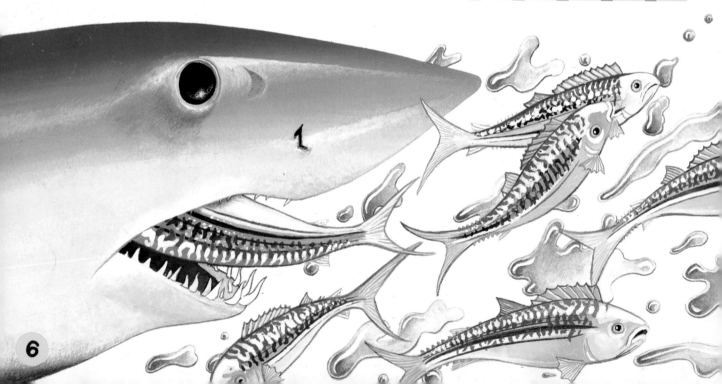

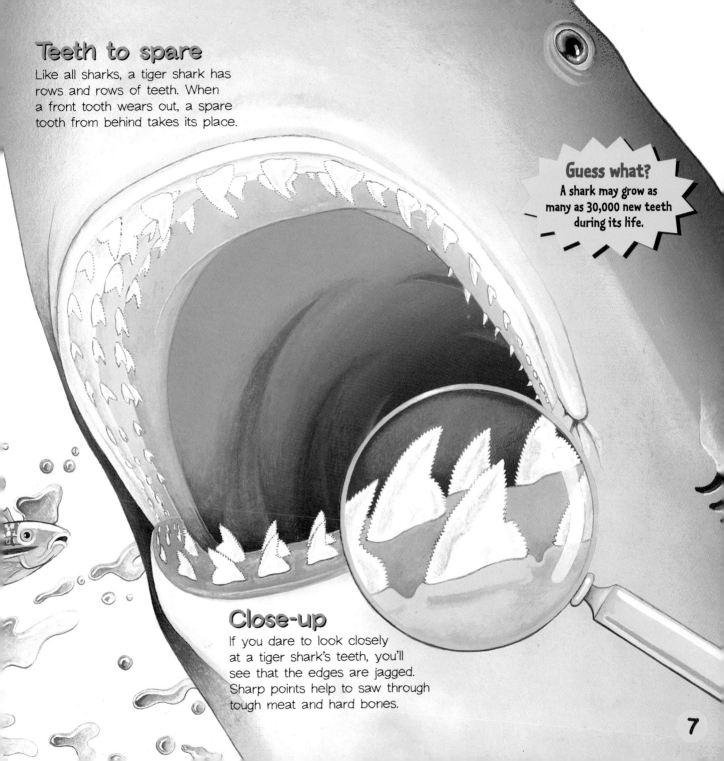

Teeth to spare

Like all sharks, a tiger shark has rows and rows of teeth. When a front tooth wears out, a spare tooth from behind takes its place.

Guess what?

A shark may grow as many as 30,000 new teeth during its life.

Close-up

If you dare to look closely at a tiger shark's teeth, you'll see that the edges are jagged. Sharp points help to saw through tough meat and hard bones.

Hammerhead shark

This shark is easy to spot because its head is the shape of the top of a hammer. A hungry hammerhead shark looks for food with its big, bulging eyes and sniffs the water with its nose.

How wide?

Stretch your arms out really wide. That's about the width of a hammerhead shark's head!

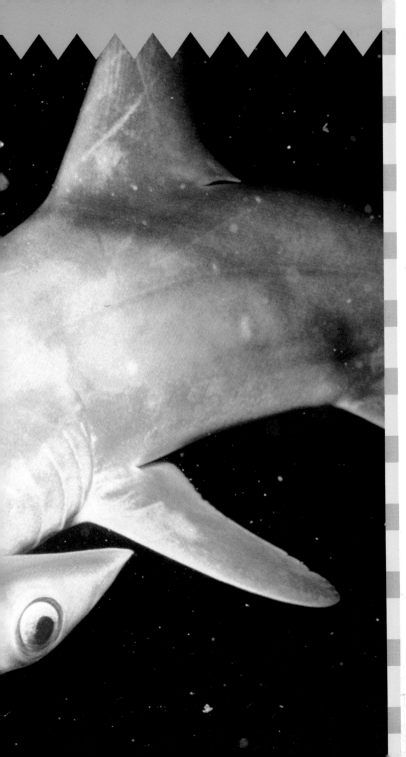

Hammerhead shark facts

Imagine being able to see things from the front and the back of your head. A hammerhead shark can!

Often, groups of hammerhead sharks swim for miles and miles through the ocean to find a new place to live.

Like all baby sharks, a baby hammerhead shark looks just like its parents, except that it's smaller.

On the hunt

A shark is an expert hunter. It races towards its prey at top speed, steering with its tail and fins. Suddenly, the shark opens its jaws and bites.

It's a knockout

A thresher shark stuns small fish by whacking them with its tail. Then the powerful shark gobbles up the dizzy fish.

Guess what?
Sharks have such sharp eyesight that they can even spot food at night.

In the nursery

Hungry sea animals like to eat little pups for their dinner, so baby sharks try to hide in safe places.

Guess what?
Lemon shark pups bite each other while they are still inside their mother.

Sharks galore

A lemon shark gives birth to about ten pups at a time. They pop out, one after the other, then the mother shark swims off without them.

Weird and wonderful

The world's strangest sharks live deep down at the bottom of the ocean. There are pink sharks, sharks with beards and even sharks that glow in the dark.

Snap it up

A wobbegong's spotted body and straggly beard help it to hide on the ocean floor. This crafty shark waits here quietly until a lobster crawls by, then it snaps up the crunchy snack.

Strange cookie

The tiny cookiecutter shark is named after the small, round bite marks it makes. They are the same shape as cookies.

Guess what?

Lots of sharks are named after other animals. How many can you find in this book?

16

Pretty strange

The pink goblin shark is the most colourful shark, but it's so rare that only a few people have ever seen it.

Monster of the deep

Megamouth lives in the deepest parts of the ocean, guzzling jellyfish and shrimps. It has a strange, monster-sized mouth that lights up in the dark.

THE TRUTH ABOUT SHARKS

Many people think that sharks are scary animals that want to gobble us up. Let's find out what sharks are really like...

1 There are 350 different types of sharks. Most of them are far more scared of you than you are of them.

Look out, she's coming towards us!

2 The biggest shark of all, the whale shark, is so gentle that you can swim alongside it.

3 Sharks don't like to eat people, but sometimes the big meat-eaters make mistakes. From below, a surfer looks just like a tasty turtle.

4 It's far more common for people to eat sharks! In Europe, shark steaks are served with chips. In Asia, shark-fin soup is a luxury.

5 Many sharks are in real danger. People have hunted so many great white sharks that there are very few left.

MKL 61

TO THE RESCUE

So, you see, sharks aren't so scary. Some countries even have laws to protect sharks in danger.

PLEASE BE NICE TO ME

Fast facts

On these pages, you can find out about your favourite sharks.

12 metres
whale shark

Great white shark

Teeth: large and jagged
Food: fish, birds and large animals such as seals.
Special body parts: huge jaws that open 90 centimetres wide.
Babies: grow inside their mother.
Amazing fact: usually swims at 3 kilometres per hour, but swims seven times faster when it's about to pounce on its dinner.

Hammerhead shark

Teeth: small and jagged
Food: fish and squid
Special body parts: a wide, flat head with eyes at the ends for seeing all around.
Babies: grow inside their mother. A baby hammerhead is born with a belly button.
Amazing fact: one of the best hunters. It even finds fish that are hiding under the sand.

Whale shark

Teeth: 15,000, and tiny
Food: tiny plankton and small fish.
Special body parts: a mouth that's wide enough for a person to fit inside.
Babies: grow inside their mother. Whale sharks are so rare that only a few babies have ever been seen.
Amazing fact: weighs more than 16 tonnes. That's more than three elephants!

20

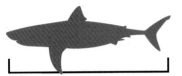
6 metres
great white shark

3.3 metres
hammerhead
shark

3 metres
wobbegong

3 metres
mako shark

1.2 metres
child

0.9 metres
dogfish

Mako shark

Teeth: long and pointed
Food: fish
Special body parts: strong muscles for swimming really quickly.
Babies: grow inside their mother. Sometimes, baby mako sharks eat each other before they are born.
Amazing fact: one of the fastest fish in the world. Its top speed is 32 kilometres per hour.

Wobbegong

Teeth: pointed at the front and flat at the back.
Food: lobsters, crabs and fish
Special body parts: long flaps of skin around its mouth, like a beard.
Babies: grow inside their mother.
Amazing fact: fish may try to nibble the shaggy beard because it looks like juicy seaweed. Then the wobbegong gobbles up the fish!

Dogfish

Teeth: small and pointed
Food: small fish and shellfish such as clams.
Special body parts: spotted skin that helps it to hide. Many bigger sea animals like to eat dogfish.
Babies: hatch from eggs in the sea. The eggshells are almost see-through.
Amazing fact: there are more dogfish in the world than any other type of shark.

Puzzles

Here are some puzzles to try. Look back in the book to help you find the answers.

Close-up!

We've zoomed in on some sharks that you met earlier. Which sharks are you looking at?

Hungry hunters

These hungry sharks are hunting for a meal. Follow the lines to find each shark's favourite food.

tiger shark

fish

blue shark

crab

angel shark

turtle

Spot the difference

Look carefully at this great white shark. Can you spot four differences between the pictures?

a

b

Who am I?

Here are shadows of three different sharks. Can you name each one?

1

2

3

Index

Created and published by
Two-Can Publishing Ltd
346 Old Street
London
EC1V 9RB

TWO CAN ™

Consultant: Dr Frances Dipper
Main illustrations: Miles Changeur
Cartoon illustrations: Alan Rowe
Photographs: front cover Natural History Photographic Agency; p4 Ardea London Ltd; p8 BBC Natural History Unit Picture Library; p12 Planet Earth Pictures.

Copyright © Golden Books Publishing Company Inc, 1998
British edition © Two-Can Publishing Ltd, 1999

'Two-Can' is a trademark of Two-Can Publishing Ltd.

ISBN 1-85434-788-8

Dewey Decimal Classification 597

Paperback 10 9 8 7 6 5 4 3 2 1

A catalogue record for this book is available from the British Library.

Printed in Hong Kong by Wing King Tong